POSITIONS ON THE TEAM

# POSITIONS IN BASEBALL

AMY B. ROGERS

PowerKiDS press

New York

Published in 2023 by The Rosen Publishing Group, Inc.
29 East 21st Street, New York, NY 10010



Portions of this work were originally authored by Ryan Nagelhout and published as *Baseball: Who Does What?* All new material in this edition was authored by Amy B. Rogers.

Editor: Katie Kawa
Book Design: Michael Flynn

Photo Credits: Cover and interior (baseball) Sanit Fuangnakhon/Shutterstock.com;(series jersey texture) Kwangmoozaa/Shutterstock.com; cover (dirt texture) Simon Tang/Shutterstock.com; cover (grass texture) comzeal images/Shutterstock.com; cover (baseball play) Dejan Popovic/Shutterstock.com; p. 5 (main) YES Market Media/Shutterstock.com; pp. 5 (inset), 22 (inset), 29 Antony McAulay/Shutterstock.com; pp. 7, 25 JoeSAPhotos/Shutterstock.com; pp. 9 (main), 11, 17 Artur Didyk/Shuttetsock.com; p. 9 (inset) Fuller Photography/Shutterstock.com; p. 13 (main) Cynthia Farmer/Shutterstock.com; p. 13 (inset) Rick Scuteri/Shutterstock.com; pp. 15, 16 (inset), 21 (main) Andrey Yurlov/Shutterstock.com; p. 19 Jamie Roach/Shutterstock.com; p. 21 (inset) Alex Kravtsov/Shutterstock.com; p. 23 Debby Wong/Shutterstock.com; p. 27 (main) Jan de Wild/Shutterstock.com; p. 27 (softball) Mtsaride/Shutterstock.com.

Library of Congress Cataloging-in-Publication Data

Names: Rogers, Amy B., author.
Title: Positions in baseball / Amy B. Rogers.
Description: New York : PowerKids Press, [2023] | Series: Positions on the team | Includes index.
Identifiers: LCCN 2021061072 | ISBN 9781538386941 (set) | ISBN 9781538386958 (library binding) | ISBN 9781538386934 (paperback) | ISBN 9781538386965 (ebook)
Subjects: LCSH: Baseball–Juvenile literature. | Major League Baseball (Organization)–Juvenile literature.
Classification: LCC GV867.5 .R65 2023 | DDC 796.357–dc23
LC record available at https://lccn.loc.gov/2021061072

Manufactured in the United States of America



CPSIA Compliance Information: Batch #CSPK23. For Further Information contact Rosen Publishing, New York, New York at 1-800-237-9932.

# CONTENTS

# PLAYING AMERICA'S PASTIME

Baseball is often called "America's Pastime." It's one of the most popular sports in the United States and in many other countries around the world too. Many kids grow up playing baseball. The best baseball players make it to the highest level of the sport in the United States: Major League Baseball (MLB).

Whether you want to make it to the MLB someday or just root for your favorite team, it helps to know as much as you can about this sport. Every player on a baseball team has a different job to do, and understanding those jobs can make playing and watching baseball even more fun!

## WHERE DID IT COME FROM?

Baseball's beginnings are hard to trace. Many different groups throughout history played games in which people had to hit a ball in a way that's similar to how baseball is played today. The rules and number of players on the field changed many times over the years until baseball as we know it today came to be.

## THINK FAST!

NINE IS AN IMPORTANT NUMBER IN BASEBALL. THERE ARE NINE PLAYERS ON A TEAM AND NINE INNINGS IN A GAME.

Baseball is a game that can change with every pitch, so every player on the field, or diamond, needs to be ready for action!

# BATTING BASICS

A baseball game starts with someone at bat, or ready to hit the ball. They're called the batter or hitter. Hitting is a hard part of a baseball player's job because everyone on the other team is working to stop the batter from getting hits—because hits can lead to runs.

The most important thing a hitter can do is see the ball. They watch either the ball itself or how a pitcher stands to figure out what kind of pitch is being thrown. Swinging the bat at the right time to get a hit takes a lot of practice!

## HARD TO HIT

Batting isn't easy. Even the best hitters in the major leagues only get a hit in 3 out of 10 at-bats. Don't worry if it seems hard to score a run–it just means the other team's players are good at their jobs! Good fielders catch even well-hit balls for outs, and pitchers often know how to trick batters into swinging at bad pitches.

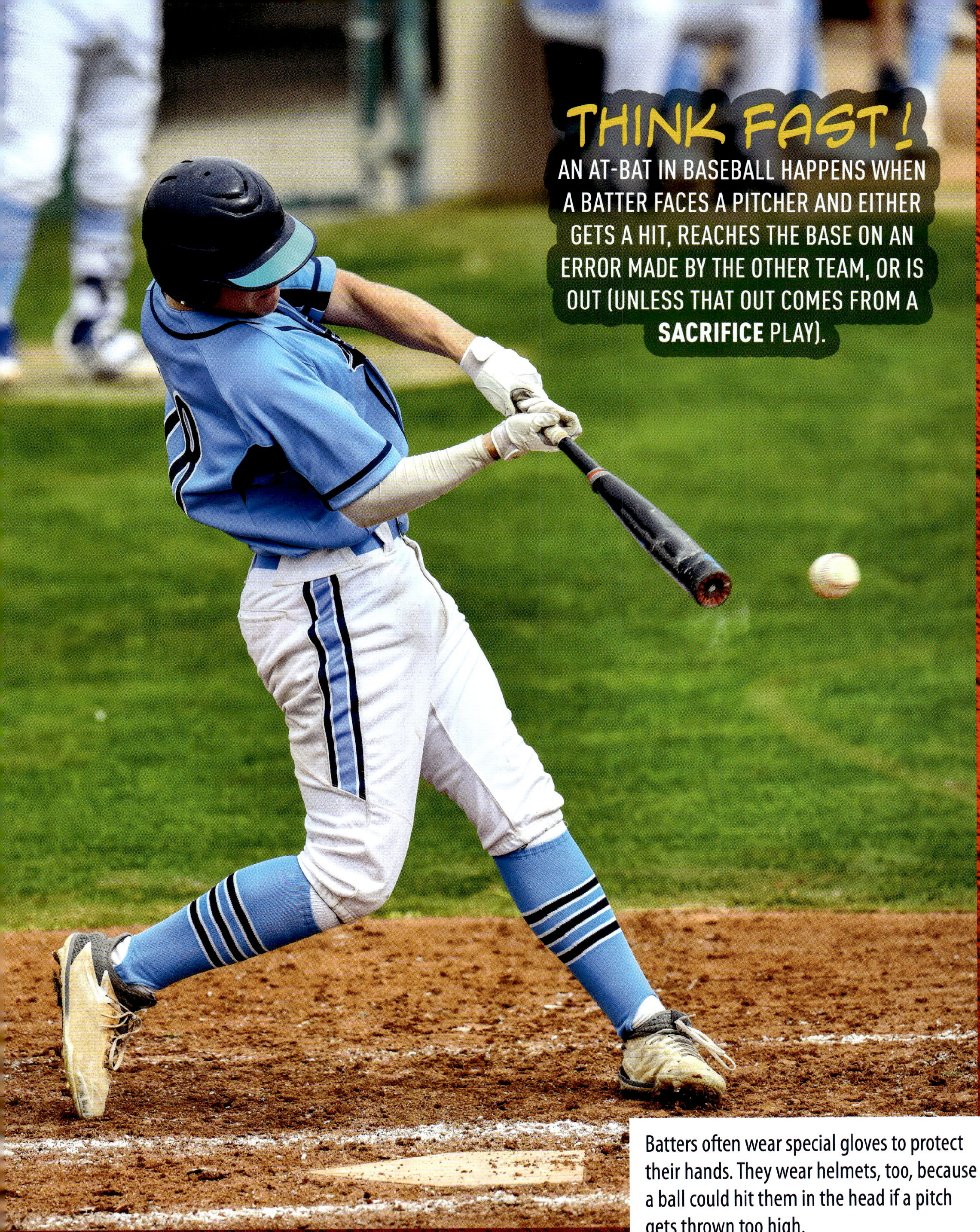

## THINK FAST!

AN AT-BAT IN BASEBALL HAPPENS WHEN A BATTER FACES A PITCHER AND EITHER GETS A HIT, REACHES THE BASE ON AN ERROR MADE BY THE OTHER TEAM, OR IS OUT (UNLESS THAT OUT COMES FROM A **SACRIFICE** PLAY).

Batters often wear special gloves to protect their hands. They wear helmets, too, because a ball could hit them in the head if a pitch gets thrown too high.

# YOU'RE OUT!

Batters don't want to strike out. When a pitch goes through the strike zone, the umpire calls it a strike—whether the batter swings at it or not. The strike zone is the space above home plate and in front of the catcher that a pitcher tries to throw the ball through. Any time a batter swings at a pitch and misses, it's also a strike.

When a batter gets three strikes, they're out. Good batters defend the strike zone, swinging at pitches in the zone while not swinging at pitches outside the zone that will be called balls.

## WHAT'S A WALK?

Batters shouldn't swing at every pitch, especially when a pitcher is missing the strike zone. If the pitcher misses the strike zone and the batter doesn't swing, it's called a ball. When a batter doesn't swing at four balls, they get to go to first base on a walk. It's often said a walk can be as good as a hit!

## THINK FAST!

THERE'S NO TIME LIMIT TO HOW LONG A BASEBALL GAME CAN LAST. AN INNING GIVES BOTH TEAMS A CHANCE TO BAT UNTIL THE DEFENDING TEAM RECORDS THREE OUTS.

It's an umpire's job to decide if a pitch is a strike or a ball.

# RUNNING THE BASES

Once a batter hits the ball, it's time to run! A hit happens when a player puts the ball in play between the **foul poles** and reaches a base before they can be thrown out.

Players are called runners when they're on base. Runners must be careful when they leave bases, or they can be tagged out. A runner is tagged out when a fielder touches them with the ball after they leave their base. If a runner touches all the bases and arrives back at home plate, a run is scored. The more runs, the better—at least for the team scoring them!

## MOVING THE RUNNERS

Sometimes a batter's job is just to move the runners to the next base. These batters often put their bats in the strike zone without swinging. Some soft hits that don't leave the infield are called bunts. When a batter bunts, they're often thrown out at first base, but the other runners get to move.

## THINK FAST!

THERE ARE FOUR DIFFERENT KINDS OF HITS IN BASEBALL. A SINGLE MOVES THE BATTER TO FIRST BASE. A DOUBLE MOVES THEM TO SECOND BASE. A TRIPLE MOVES THEM TO THIRD BASE, AND A HOME RUN TAKES THEM PAST THOSE THREE BASES AND BACK TO HOME PLATE.

Did you know it's a good thing to steal in baseball? When a runner goes to the next base before or during a pitch, this is called stealing a base. The base can't have another player on it, though!

# THE PERFECT PITCH

When a team isn't batting, their job is to keep the team that is from scoring. Everyone has a different job to do to make that happen. A pitcher's job is to throw strikes and get the other team's batters out. Often, they do this by throwing a fastball—a pitch that comes in hard and fast.

Pitchers also have other pitches they can use to make batters strike out. A curve ball dips and drops through the strike zone. A changeup looks like a fastball but is thrown much slower. This makes a batter swing too early. Pitchers have to practice just like batters do.

## MORE THAN ONE PITCHER

A pitcher's arm often gets tired as the game goes on. Because of this, teams often use different pitchers throughout a baseball game. Pitchers who come in later in a game are called relief pitchers. A closer is a relief pitcher who comes in to get the final outs of the game.

## THINK FAST!

MLB PITCHERS CAN THROW A BASEBALL MORE THAN 100 MILES (161 KM) PER HOUR!

Many pitchers have one kind of pitch they're better at than others. Each kind of pitch calls for a different grip on the baseball.

# BEHIND THE PLATE

Pitchers aren't alone when facing a batter. They work with the catcher to figure out what pitches might work best to get each batter out. Catchers **crouch** down behind home plate and use different fingers to signal to the pitcher what they should throw.

That's not all a catcher does! Catchers try to keep pitches from getting behind them. Sometimes a catcher will block a wild pitch in the dirt or have to throw all the way to second base on a stolen base attempt. They also have to protect home plate. This means tagging out a runner trying to score by touching home plate.

## KEEPING CATCHERS SAFE

If you've ever seen a catcher, you know they wear a lot of gear. Their job is very hard, and they often get hit by the ball. They wear special guards for their legs and a chest protector. They also wear a helmet with a mask to protect their face.

## THINK FAST!

A CATCHER USES A SPECIAL KIND OF GLOVE CALLED A MITT.

Catchers have to study hard! They often watch film, or videos, of the other team's hitters before a game so they know what kinds of pitches to call.

# FIRST THINGS FIRST

First base sees a lot of action in a baseball game. The first baseman's job is to catch any ball thrown their way to get a batter out at first base. Defensive plays on **ground balls** often end with another infielder throwing to the first baseman.

## A GOOD PLACE FOR LEFTIES

People who throw with their left hand often play first base. This is because they don't have to make tough throws to their left, which is harder for them to do. First basemen who wear their glove on their right hand also can more easily **snag** balls hit between first and second base.

To make the out, the first baseman puts one foot on the base, then leans toward the person throwing the ball to catch it as soon as possible. They have to keep their foot on the base while they catch the ball. If the ball gets in their glove before the runner gets to first base, the runner is out.

## THINK FAST!

LIKE A CATCHER, A FIRST BASEMAN WEARS A SPECIAL KIND OF GLOVE. THIS KIND OF GLOVE MAKES IT EASIER TO CATCH ALL THE BALLS THROWN THEIR WAY.

A first baseman sometimes has to stretch very far to make a catch while keeping their foot on the base.

# TURNING TWO

If you play second base, you don't actually spend a lot of time there! A second baseman often plays between first and second base and waits for balls hit between the bases. They make diving stops and throw the ball to first base for outs.

A second baseman can make an out at second base too. They can get a runner out as they go from first to second base after a hit. Sometimes, they'll then throw the ball to first base to get the hitter out too. That's called a double play. Second basemen often need to quickly cover a lot of ground.

## MAKING A CHOICE

Second basemen have to think quickly. They need to know where runners are on the bases and if they're trying to advance along the base paths or even score. Sometimes a fielder will throw to second or third base instead of throwing to first to get a runner out. This is known as a fielder's choice.

## THINK FAST!

MAKING A DOUBLE PLAY IS SOMETIMES CALLED "TURNING TWO."

Having a quick body and a quick mind are important if you want to play second base.

# THE HOT CORNER

If you have a strong arm, third base might be the place for you! Third basemen have to throw all the way across the diamond to beat runners down the first base line to record outs.

Third basemen sometimes play close to the base, especially when their **opponent** has a runner on third. They also might field bunts down the third base line, which doesn't give them much time to make a good throw to a base. This means third basemen often make off-balance throws in a hurry. They have to be strong and **accurate** with their throws to get an out.

## TOO HOT?

Third basemen often play closer to the batter than anyone else on the field besides the catcher. Hits to this position often come very quickly off right-handed batters. A third baseman needs to have quick **reflexes** to not only catch the ball, but also to stay safe. This is why third base is known as the "hot corner."

## THINK FAST!

THIRD BASEMEN SOMETIMES HAVE TO CATCH LINE DRIVES, WHICH ARE HITS THAT TRAVEL IN A STRAIGHT LINE NOT TOO FAR INTO THE AIR. LINE DRIVES CAN BE HIT VERY HARD!

It's good for a third baseman to be brave!

# WHAT'S A SHORTSTOP?

A shortstop generally plays between second and third base. They're some of the best **athletes** on the field and have to cover the most ground in the infield. The shortstop often turns double plays at second base and can cover the base when a catcher throws to second on a stolen base attempt.

## NUMBERS ON THE DIAMOND

Each defensive position on a baseball diamond has its own number. The shortstop is number 6, after the pitcher, catcher, and first, second, and third basemen. The left fielder is 7, center fielder is 8, and right fielder is number 9. This makes it quick and easy to write down who made an out.

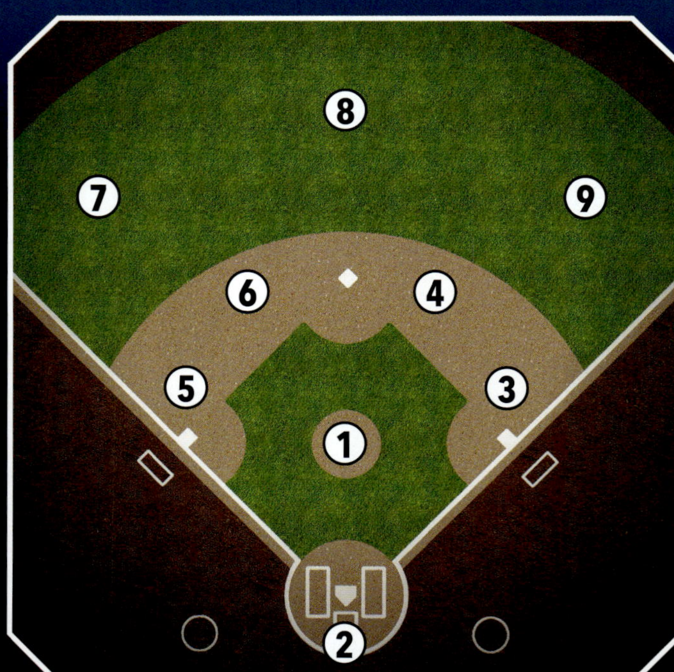

A shortstop tells other infielders where to position themselves on the field for certain batters. They're often very smart players with very good reflexes. Shortstops are known as the captains of the infield because they help control the way their team is playing from the field.

## THINK FAST!

THE INFIELD IS THE AREA OF THE BASEBALL DIAMOND BETWEEN THE THREE BASES AND HOME PLATE. IT'S OFTEN COVERED WITH DIRT, WHILE THE OUTFIELD IS OFTEN GRASS.

One of the most famous shortstops in MLB history is Derek Jeter. He played for the New York Yankees from 1995 to 2014 and won five World Series titles.

# LEFT, RIGHT, CENTER

The players in the infield all have their own important roles, or jobs, on a baseball team. The same is true for the players in the outfield. There are three different outfield positions: center fielder, left fielder, and right fielder. Their names come from where they stand in the outfield.

Center field is considered the hardest of these positions. Center fielders cover the most area in the outfield, so they have to be fast and able to make diving catches. All outfielders need to have a strong arm to throw the ball to the infielders and stop hits from becoming runs.

## I GOT IT!

Outfielders often have to catch fly balls—balls hit very high in the air. This isn't easy! Outfielders have to read the path of a ball to get under it and catch it. Sometimes, more than one player might be tracking a fly ball. When this happens, one player needs to say, "I got it!"

## THINK FAST!

OUTFIELDERS ALSO NEED TO BACK UP ANOTHER FIELDER TRYING TO MAKE A DIVING PLAY ON A BALL IN CASE THEY MISS IT.

Outfield positions are just as important as infield ones. A talented group of outfielders can make a baseball team very successful.

# WHAT ABOUT SOFTBALL?

Learning about all the positions on the diamond can help you understand baseball better, and it can also help you understand softball. This is a sport that's very similar to baseball. In fact, it has all the same positions.

The biggest difference between softball and baseball is the way the pitcher throws the ball. Baseball pitchers throw overhand, while softball pitchers throw underhand. There are also two types of softball: slow-pitch and fast-pitch. In slow-pitch softball, there are typically 10 players on each team. The extra player is often in the outfield. Fast-pitch softball typically has nine players on a team.

## WOMEN IN BASEBALL

Fast-pitch softball is often played by women. However, women can play baseball too. There are no rules that say any baseball position can only be played by a man. In fact, many kids play on baseball teams with both boys and girls. Young women also play on college baseball teams. Baseball is a sport for everyone!

The positions on a fast-pitch softball team are the same as the ones on a baseball team.

## THINK FAST!

A SOFTBALL IS LARGER AND HEAVIER THAN A BASEBALL.

# MORE TO LEARN

Now you know the basics of baseball positions, but how can you learn more? Watch how the **professionals** in the MLB play. Pay attention to what bases players cover on what kinds of plays. For example, when a first baseman has to cover a ground ball, sometimes the pitcher covers first base for them.

When you're learning to play baseball, it can be both fun and helpful to try playing many different positions. This can help you learn where your favorite place to play is on the diamond. It's helpful to know the facts about each position so you can play them safely and successfully!

## A DIFFERENT LOOK

The job of each player doesn't always stay the same throughout a baseball game. Sometimes the entire infield changes when a certain kind of batter comes to the plate. This is called "The Shift." Some left-handed hitters will see a third baseman shift over to play shortstop, who shifts to play between first and second. Then, the second baseman plays shallow right field.

## THINK FAST!

LITTLE LEAGUE BASEBALL AND SOFTBALL IS THE LEADING ORGANIZATION FOR YOUTH BASEBALL AND SOFTBALL IN THE UNITED STATES AND AROUND THE WORLD. MILLIONS OF KIDS PLAY ON LITTLE LEAGUE TEAMS.

Shown here are all the positions on a baseball team. Which one seems like the most fun to you?

# GLOSSARY

**accurate:** Free from mistakes; able to hit the target.

**athlete:** A person who plays a sport.

**crouch:** To stoop or bend low with the arms and legs close to the body.

**foul pole:** A pole, netting, line, or other indicator of whether or not a ball passing above the outfield fence is fair or foul.

**ground ball:** A hit in baseball that rolls along the ground.

**opponent:** A member of the other team in a game.

**professional:** A person who does a job that requires special skill.

**reflex:** An action or movement of the body that happens automatically as a reaction to something.

**sacrifice:** Referring to a play in baseball (most often a bunt) that allows a runner to advance one base while the batter is put out.

**snag:** To catch something by reaching out quickly.

# FOR MORE INFORMATION

## BOOKS

Beattie, Amy. *What Is Baseball?* New York, NY: Britannica Educational Publishing, 2019.

Small, Cathleen. *Baseball.* New York, NY: Gareth Stevens Publishing, 2019.

Velasco, Catherine Ann. *Behind the Scenes of Pro Baseball.* North Mankato, MN: Capstone Press, 2019.

## WEBSITES

**Baseball Glossary**
*mlb.com/glossary*
Read all about special terms used in baseball and what they mean here.

**Baseball Hall of Fame**
*baseballhall.org*
Learn about the greatest players of all time at each position when you visit the official website of the Baseball Hall of Fame.

**Little League Baseball and Softball**
*www.littleleague.org*
Visitors to this website can learn more about Little League teams in their community and around the world.

**Publisher's note to educators and parents:** Our editors have carefully reviewed these websites to ensure that they are suitable for students. Many websites change frequently, however, and we cannot guarantee that a site's future contents will continue to meet our high standards of quality and educational value. Be advised that students should be closely supervised whenever they access the internet.

# INDEX